First Facts®

Transportation Zone

Bulldozers

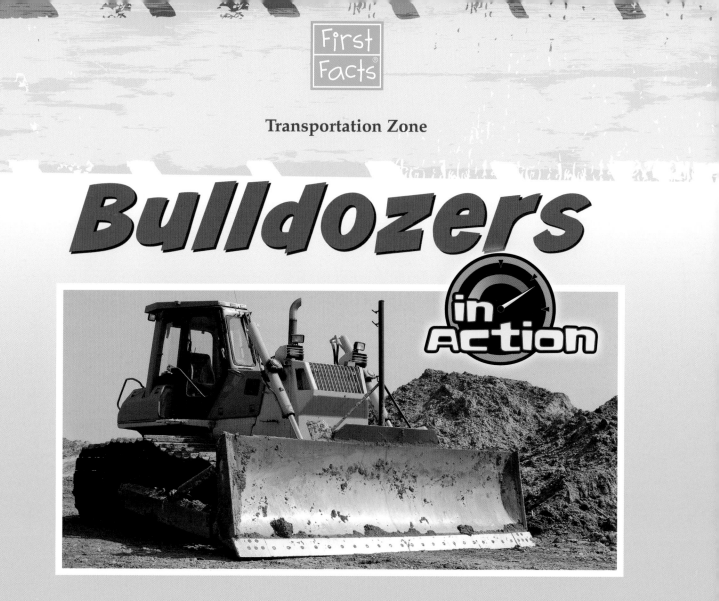

in Action

by Peter Brady

CAPSTONE PRESS
a capstone imprint

First Facts is published by Capstone Press,
1710 Roe Crest Drive, North Mankato, Minnesota 56003.
www.capstonepub.com

Books published by Capstone Press are manufactured with paper
containing at least 10 percent post-consumer waste.

Library of Congress Cataloging-in-Publication Data
Brady, Peter, 1944 Sept. 22–
  Bulldozers in action / by Peter Brady.
     p. cm. — (First facts. Transportation zone)
  Includes bibliographical references and index.
  Summary: "Describes bulldozers, including their history, their parts, and how they
work"—Provided by publisher.
  ISBN 978-1-4296-7692-2 (library binding)
  ISBN 978-1-4296-7965-7 (paperback)
  1. Bulldozers—Juvenile literature. I. Title. II. Series.
  TA735.B68 2012
  629.225—dc23   2011029171

Editorial Credits
Carrie Braulick Sheely, editor; Sarah Bennett and Lori Bye, designers;
    Eric Gohl, media researcher; Kathy McColley, production specialist

Image Credits
Alamy/Florida Images, 6; photosilta, 14; Robert Shantz, 10
Capstone Studio/Karon Dubke, 13, 22
Getty Images/Fox Photos, 16
iStockphoto/Martin Wahlborg, 5; Tracy Fox, cover
Public Domain, 21 (top)
Shutterstock/J van der Wolf, 9; Jan van Broekhoven, 1, 21 (bottom); Lou Oates, 19

Printed in the United States of America in North Mankato, Minnesota.

102011   006405CGS12

Table of Contents

Bulldozers

A bulldozer's huge blade digs into the dirt. The vehicle moves forward, pushing the dirt into a pile. Next the bulldozer shoves a huge rock aside. Soon the cleared area will become a new road.

Bulldozers are earthmovers. They push dirt and scrape the ground. They are often the first machines used to build a road or building.

Bulldozer Parts

The main part of a bulldozer is the large front blade. The blade is made of heavy steel.

Some bulldozers run on wheels. But most bulldozers move using wide **tracks**. The tracks let the bulldozer work in muddy areas where wheels would sink. They also help a bulldozer travel over rough ground.

> **track:** a long belt that stretches around small wheels on a vehicle; an engine powers the wheels to make the track turn

Types of Blades

The type of blade a bulldozer uses depends on its job. Short, straight blades help bulldozers smooth out land. Tall, curved blades push large amounts of dirt. Blade wings help hold materials in front of a bulldozer.

wing

9

ripper

Extra Equipment

Bulldozers often have extra equipment for tough jobs. Some have a metal spike on the back called a ripper. The ripper breaks up hard ground.

Some bulldozer tracks are covered with raised steel pieces. These pieces are called spurs. Spurs help break up dirt as the vehicle moves.

How a Bulldozer Works

A bulldozer has many controls in the cab. The driver uses a handle to move the blade. The blade is powered by **hydraulics**. A **throttle** controls the bulldozer's speed.

Drivers use hand levers or foot pedals to control a bulldozer with tracks. The right and left tracks are controlled separately. This feature allows the bulldozer to turn.

hydraulics: a system powered by fluid forced through pipes or chambers

throttle: a lever that controls the flow of fuel into the engine

Where Bulldozers Work

Bulldozers work at many types of **construction sites**. The machines level out ground. They remove tree stumps where homes and roads are being built. Bulldozers also move dirt at **quarries** and coal mines. Some bulldozers bury and move garbage at landfills.

construction site: a place where something is being built

quarry: a place where stone or other minerals are dug from the ground

15

Early Bulldozers

Nobody knows who invented the first bulldozer powered by an engine. But large blades similar to a bulldozer's were used in the 1800s. Mules pushed these blades around.

In the early 1900s, people started putting blades on tractors. These vehicles were the first bulldozers. Over time, bulldozers improved. By the 1940s, they used hydraulics.

Working as a Team

A bulldozer often works with other vehicles. These machines include backhoes, dump trucks, and graders. A bulldozer pushes dirt into big piles. Backhoes scoop up the dirt. They load the dirt into dump trucks. The trucks then carry the dirt away. Graders smooth out the ground. Wherever they work, bulldozers get the job done.

Bulldozer Facts

- The word "bulldozer" used to describe only the vehicle's blade.

- The U.S. military uses bulldozers for clearing pathways, construction, and other jobs. Some of these bulldozers have armor to protect the drivers from attacks.

- Some bulldozers are operated by remote control.

- Bulldozers with tracks are sometimes called crawler tractors.

- Japanese manufacturer Komatsu made the largest factory-built bulldozer. It stands 16 feet (4.9 meters) tall and is 38.5 feet (11.7 meters) long. Komatsu named it the Super Dozer.

Komatsu Super Dozer

Hands On: Bulldozer Blades

A bulldozer has different blades depending on its job. Find out how different blades work as they push through dirt.

What You Need

a large piece of strong cardboard
scissors
ruler

masking tape
a pile of sand or loose dirt, at least 3 inches (7.6 cm) deep

What You Do

1. Cut a rectangle out of the cardboard that is 5 inches (12.7 cm) wide and 2 inches (5 cm) tall. This will be your straight blade.
2. Cut another rectangle that is 6 inches (15 cm) wide and 4 inches (10 cm) tall. This will be your curved blade.
3. Cut two pieces of cardboard that are 2 inches (5 cm) wide and 4 inches (10 cm) tall. These will be your bulldozer wings.
4. Now experiment with how your blades work in the sand. Slowly move your straight blade through the sand. Notice how the blade levels the sand as it moves. Now take your second piece of cardboard. Squeeze both the top and bottom to make the cardboard curve slightly. Then move it through the sand. Did this blade scoop up more dirt than your straight blade? Finally, tape a wing onto each short end of the second blade. The wings should stick out straight forward. Do these wings help keep the dirt on the blade?

Glossary

cab (KAB)— an area for a driver to sit in a large truck or machine

construction site (kuhn-STRUHKT-shuhn SYT)—a place where something is built, such as roads or buildings

hydraulics (hye-DRAW-liks)—a system powered by fluid forced through pipes or chambers

quarry (KWOR-ee)—a place where stone or other minerals are dug from the ground

throttle (THROT-uhl)—a lever that controls how much fuel and air flow into an engine; the throttle controls the speed of a vehicle

track (TRAK)—a belt that some vehicles travel on; the track wraps around small wheels that are powered by an engine

Read More

Addison, D. R. *Bulldozers at Work*. Big Trucks. New York: PowerKids Press, 2009.

Gillis, Jennifer Blizin. *The World's Dirtiest Machines*. Extreme Machines. Chicago: Raintree, 2011.

Tourville, Amanda Doering. *Bulldozers*. Mighty Machines. Edina, Minn.: Magic Wagon, 2009.

Internet Sites

FactHound offers a safe, fun way to find Internet sites related to this book. All of the sites on FactHound have been researched by our staff.

Here's all you do:

Visit *www.facthound.com*

Type in this code: 9781429676922

 Check out projects, games and lots more at **www.capstonekids.com**

Index